BEYOND NURSERY RHYMES;

Real Life Tales

Shantelle 'Elle' McLin

GENERAL INFORMATION

Beyond Nursery Rhymes;

Real Life Tales

By

Shantelle 'Elle' McLin

2nd Edition: 2020

Interior Design by

CTU

Publishing Group

a division of Creative Talents Unleashed
www.creativetalentsunleashed.com

ISBN: 9798644567577

Credits

Book Cover

Raja Williams

Book Description

Brenda-Lee Ranta

Editor

Shantelle 'Elle' McLin

Foreword

Tonya Allen

Dedication

I dedicate this book to the wearied, shaken and lost souls that are searching for a glimpse of light. Our life challenges aren't to control us but mold us. Our trials in life are not to stunt, but to elevate us as we evolve from life's pupils into life's teachers. We are not our past, we have the amazing ability to move forward even with the most complex personal histories. It is how we deal with our personal pain that creates a fine line between suffering and living.

Foreword

Author Shantelle McLin's extraordinary talent leaves me in awe. She can make words jump, turn, spin and plié. They bend at her will. She is a language contortionist. Her words are pained, pulled and stretched into creating an experience both truthful and beautiful. Such a talent is rare. Such a talent is nurtured. Such talent is praised. Such praise is earned. Such praise is deserved for *Beyond Nursery Rhymes.*

Nursery rhymes are poems and songs used to teach and entertain young children. In McLin's collection, there are no "to market, to market" or "cock a doodle doos." Rather, she crafts a uniquely adult experience through her work that cajoles her readers into the full experience of adulthood. McLin reveals both darkness and light, despair and hope, and love and hate in ways that are truthful, authentic and transparent to the human experience. If music and rhyme increase a child's ability in spatial reasoning and aid in their development, then McLin's work matures and perfects the ability of adults to face their realities with grace, strength, and love.

Beyond Nursery Rhymes provides its readers with a collection of poems that cultivate more developed and complex imagery and narrative about life. In many ways, her collection, like nursery rhymes, mimics the love of tragedy, which invokes in its audience catharsis, drama, pleasure, and a paradoxical response. McLin takes universal themes that are well represented in traditional nursery rhymes, shows conflicting sides, and presents them in a more contemporary context. Here is a set of examples.

Humpty Dumpty had a great fall. In *Self Destruction* and *My Scars*, McLin openly shares defeat and brokenness in the public domain, which is reminiscent of Humpty Dumpty's fall and the inability of the king's men to put him back together again. McLin's work shares that true repair cannot be accomplished through the effort of others, but rather through one's own self-reflection, honesty, and plight for healing.

And Jill came tumbling after. Jill loved Jack so much that she went up when water is normally found downhill. McLin shows the seductive and misleading, yet powerful and passionate power of love in her collection. These themes are examined in *Your Lies* and *Read My Mind Part III*. The reader has a tactile response to the dimension of love expressed in these poems.

She had so many children, she didn't know what to do. McLin's *Dear Sweet Darling* poetically captures the classic themes of responsibility, love, and despair that the Old Woman Who Lived in a Shoe experienced when she couldn't feed her children. McLin's poem queries, "Why does mommy cry?" which captures the same sentiment of despair when you can't give your children what they need, despite your best intentions.

He's under a haystack fast asleep. McLin's daring declaration, "scratching off other's expectations with my sharpie" shows that sometimes you should care for self and your needs must come first despite your responsibilities and the broader demands of the world. Like Little Boy Blue,

McLin's words in *Not a Pessimist* stake value and strength in self-care and meeting one's own personal needs.

Why, Mary loves the lamb, you know. McLin captures the full spectrum of love in several of her pieces. In *Love Visage*, McLin writes, "Cause love is music on its own," which captures the sinuous nature of love's movement. In *I love My Ugly* and *Me, Myself and I*, McLin capture the importance of self-love and embracing the complexity of your being to truly find understanding, peace, and happiness. Throughout McLin's collection, you find that she is retelling Mary Had a Little Lamb's core lesson—that love attracts love.

Simply said, Mother Goose has nothing on McLin. McLin is a talented, truthful poetess, with an amazing ability to transport you through her words. After reading *Beyond Nursery Rhymes*, you will be completely satisfied and exposed. Your experience will be aptly and concisely wrapped up and articulated in four of the nine lines composing *Poetic Affair*.

"the birth of a melodic concoction

forms a brew of passion

a love dance is inspired

songs of the soul transpired"

On a personal note, this amazing author, Shantelle McLin is my sister. I have seen the growth in her work and have witnessed her toil to perfect and mature her craft. To write a foreword for her is such an honored and challenging task, because I hope to capture words that encompass my honest respect for her work, doesn't pale in contrast to her genius and shows my breathing, palpable love for the author.

Lastly, I leave you with words directly from McLin in Divinity's Pull. *"Softer thoughts greet me this morn; My inner voice whispers reasoning; Says to me... give birth; Labor unto the world your gift. Share your shine."* And to that, I say, "Thank God, she listened, thank God she shared."

Tonya Allen, a serial "idea-preneur," serves as the Skillman Foundation's president & chief executive officer.

Preface

I believe there is something of splendor within my pain. The motivation it inspires, the undetected strength being revealed, the hope it births inside to the creativity it cultivates. Although agonizing to endure such unbearable suffering within my life, random isolated moments of peace are valued and never taken for granted. There is something quite surrendering and comforting when induced from a poetic inebriation. To become frozen within time, to nurse yourself to health in that venting moment with pen in hand it becomes a form of freedom. That moment you get to let go of the pain, right there on paper.

Suffered as I did, I have rediscovered who I am time and time again. In constant search of my purpose, I've learned to dissect life and to reveal its hidden treasures. My downfalls would not be the end of me but my rebirth. My poetry is so important to that process. It is the course of healing and dealing while constantly maturing resultantly.

The light of my path has always been my faith and surviving with pen in hand. I've learned to deal with trying times and what seems as an unfair hand dealt channeling through my grandmother's strength. I'm not unmindful that I am not alone in pain. It is others that motivate my pen. If my dark path could lead you into the direction of LIGHT then I am blessed three times over.

Although most poems scribed in this poetry book takes on a darker tone it is not for the sake of gaining compassion, but to bring awareness. In silence, we are imprisoned, both voicing and confronting our pain makes way for freedom. If we leave it hidden it becomes a spiraling tornado that brings chaos inside. If brave enough to release it, we also discharge its power and hold over us.

In this collection of semi-autobiographical book of poetry, you will hear a variety of tones. From the voice of blaring chaos inside a victim's mind, depressive cries, whispers of a lost soul searching and to the intense vibrated melodies of heart rhythms in love. I welcome you inside this wandering troubled mind that has finally found its peace. Experience the journey of life being beyond nursery rhymes!

Table of Contents

Table of Contents

Table of Contents

Table of Contents

BEYOND NURSERY RHYMES;

Real Life Tales

Shantelle 'Elle' McLin

Beautiful

Beautiful is the one who bares their soul
Allowing their essence to be seen in the dark
Their flaws are accentuated through pores,
Magnified are the defects of all impurities
And yet true substance amazes in subtleness

Beautiful is the one who blesses the soul
With the presence of an anointed spirit,
True kindness spreads through their human wings
Their voices are delicate as a song from a dove
Their deeds are unselfish and heart-pure

Beautiful is the one who is not seen nor heard
Although their presence is always sensed
An angel grounded here on earth
One who does not conform to the laws of the soil
While maintaining a strong neck from a raised head

Beautiful is the one not shamed
Acknowledging that we are not our experiences
We are the product of
We are to be built to be broken
To be remodeled and rebirthed in divine presence

YES... beautiful, are the ones reflected in our mirrors
The ones who questions our image daily
And the one who is not afraid to bare it all,
That has been freed from hiding it all
Beautiful is the one who accepts and moves onward

Pay It Forward!

As I develop, transforming my heart and mind
My spirit caresses my intentions
This new mold takes form

Coiled and curving, detailed into fine design
For once, I feel complete... whole,
This shining new presence includes a smile
Now brightened eyes

Despair, no longer here, no longer present
Sadness, still in rear view distance,
The reminder of this journey

I've fought to be here so many times,
Where glimpse could be seen,
And in trials that never had extensions
It came so fleetingly...

Kept eyes glued to this vision,
Knowing it was in reach, this feeling...
While maintaining a strong fight,
I've battled both myself and the world
Combating these evil spirits to let loose of my emotions
This smile is my victory!

Deserved,
These merited wings!
Once, a struggling existence gasping for life's air
Now I inhale the purest form of this world's oxygen,

Releasing positive energy through my exhale,
Because I know this story does not end here

Perhaps midway within my living
For no one truly knows their ending number
I feel I have so much work to do to pay it forward,
And never have I been happier to labor

I know what it's like to smother in one's own breath
To suffocate from life's air
And still, have no choice but to breathe in toxins
And now...
My lungs, know what it means to function flawlessly
To exercise its role and purpose
From Divine's guidance

I am a TESTIMONY,
I've died both literally and figuratively
Apart of me was called Home
And the remainder, that is left... has a duty
I Have A Responsibility,
Although obligated,
It gives me nothing but pure pleasure and joy

I was once hopeless
And to the world, I was helpless
But look at me now!

I've been written off... forgotten!

Told I couldn't survive,
And that statistics were not in my favor...
But look at me... do you see ME?

I am God's Creation

Transformed... both heart and mind
As my spirit caresses my intentions
This new mold takes form...

I Am Here For a REASON!

I feel I have so much work to do to pay it forward,
And never have I been happier, to labor

Mercy's River

Cobwebs have been wiped from the non-usage of my heart
Dusting clean the coverage that made me so emotionless
No more of its acquaintance to darkness
My refusal to lie in a miserable state of being

Galloping to a once far away land
As I squish my toes in the sand of peace
The shoreline ripples and cleanses the dirtiness of trotting feet
A slow jog becomes a relay race of hope

Where I once was not able to walk so I crawled my way to stronger faith
In any way, necessary, I would have reached this LIGHT
And now I find myself at mercy's river washing away layers

How many times have I become this soiled being?
Contaminated by the worldliness of earth's clay
Freedom is not a state of mind... it is a state of being
My free will have detoured me to the rocky shore

Bruised and bloodied feet know there is healing in the water
My mucky thoughts want to be cleansed
My muddied soul wants purification
Purging by sins confessed...

There is healing in HIS name

Washed clean from timeworn sin
I was reborn at this place... at mercy's river

Falling Gracefully

Today I sat under the pear tree
Leaned my back against its trunk
Propped up my legs and spilled inside my journal

The autumn chill felt much like winter
I wrote carefully my thoughts as they consumed my mind
Thinking seemed to be one tracked
"How to undo this web of mess I've begun"

The fervor of rage has taken my peace
Replaced it with fumes of detestation
Breeding inside was a declared destruction
For once,
I saw outside myself, to look inward

Epiphanies weren't new ideas
Just the old worn ignored thoughts that were newly dressed
As I sat and pondered,
The road to hell seemed closer than I desired
It seems I have traveled this back alley for some time

The tunnel I chose as a short cut brought me closer to
dysfunction
With my face cupped in my hands, newer embarrassment
formed
"Shame on Me"
You were raised better, have a relationship with the
Almighty stronger than ever
So how do you allow yourself to get here?

How?

Warring myself to ward off my inner evil...
Face, it!!!
You aren't the portrayal that others claimed you to be
Yet, suddenly, you decide to prove them, right?
What kind of hell you done dropped yourself into?

Hell?

I was harder on myself than ever
Words dropped onto the paper in fury, I was having a
conversation with myself
Well overdue…
Past overdue…
But was I listening?

The wind shook the leaves, they fell upon the pages
I sat there to stare
First fleetingly
I then became focused with one leaf
I studied it front and back
The crisp and dying edges, the three in one coloring

The way it fell wasn't a plummeting fall upon my lap
It fell gracefully
Floating until it reached a safer haven
Carrying with it… a message

Ah, now I see,
I turned the page in my journal and I paused for a long
moment
Seems like hours which only transferred into reality time…
a few brief seconds

Sometimes we fall so we can get back up…
But when you do, don't plunge hard, don't hurt yourself
Fall with some grace and dignity…
Then GET UP!

No, that leaf will never get back up,
Perhaps turn into fertilizer for the soil of the earth
In an instance, a rebirth
A reincarnation of some sort
A recycled existence
Then again, maybe its purpose was fulfilled
Just by falling upon my lap…
To direct me to my purpose!

Carla

I remember when I first saw her,
I had prejudice written across my heart
I had already formed an opinion about who she was
And what she would be to me

She didn't even appear as all the rest,
I ignored her aura just as quickly as I dismissed her
It was strange how I wouldn't notice her beauty
For my eyes already held a tainted view

I met her today,
Pretty pecan skin mixed with a hint of cream,
Short coiled curls and in a stylish vintage print A-line skirt,
Her voice calm and full of spirit

I watched as her eyes widen during our acquaintance,
See, in her field, she met many
All walks of life, all colors, all different personalities…
But I was a first

Perhaps we both were prejudging,
I imagined my eyes having the same widened affect
I could tell she admire my honesty,
Probably the first to truly appreciate it

I knew by now I had intrigued her,
Igniting inside a curiosity,
Sort of like a good book you just can't put down
You just gotta know what's coming next

And now she was a part of this story
Perhaps an intricate part of the plot
I'm aware that she could influence the ending
Or perhaps inspire a sequel maybe even a series

She was a brown eyed woman,
Who was afraid to turn the page without understanding
I appreciate that she never drew herself into a conclusion
As her patience inspired me not to write one

Dead Souls

If dead souls had life,
I'd imagine it would be like my old existence
Tired and ragged
Depletion beyond man's definition
A struggling ambition
Where there is waiting for the fruits to bear

I'd imagine their hearts bending to mend
Or needing a spiritual transfusion
To put fire on the cold inside
Where the burnt-out souls reside
Gasping for freedom's air

If dead souls cared
Perhaps love's meaning would repair
A heart that's barely there
Reviving with instruments that are winded
Propelling passion into a deflated essence
Flaring signals back into its eyes

I'd imagine something there nudging
Restoring within rather deepened
Controlling repulsion's outrage
Enslaved and encaged in rotted age
Where since felt of disposal

If dead souls had life
I'd imagine it being a horrid site
Terror in aura beyond the night

A switched off light
A mind standing still in bleakness
As love remains its kryptonite

Chancing

If I knew how to love any other way,
Would I instill in myself another's reaction to love's
action?
Would I create a balance between art and mathematics…?
Would love to become a study rather than a sculpture of
mankind fusing?
Would it be divisions and multiplications, addition and
subtraction of hesitation?
I don't know!

Could love ever to be defined? And if so, it's redefining
every day
In love, I want to become the clay…
Mold me!
Make bold of my heart!
Bravery is the only way love can start…
And even greater courage is needed for a restart

If I knew beforehand that the pain secedes,
Would I trust my instinct and proceed?
Or take heed?
Yet continue cautiously because love is not a want, but a
need

Honestly…

If I knew that doubt could erase promises
Heartache could injure souls,
While precious memories of euphoria take hold of me…

Would that still make bold of me?
Could I trust myself to feelings?

Love can never be under new management,
Because love can never be managed… yet it can damage
In love, you must succumb…
Surrender,
To experience it

Love…
You should allow it to be
Love is powerful, within its own desires, it receives
In the palest moon of night, it deceives…
And ever so trusting, it believes

If I knew that I could dangle my legs a little,
Allow them to grow numb until a deciding factor…
Maybe I would jump that fence
As I continue to try to make sense, of love…
I reach incompetence

I guess my perception will always be unsure
I can get my feet wet at the shorelines,
While making pretty hearts in the sand
Or take a chance off land, and ride the waves
With a possibility of a wipeout
But all in all, that is what love is about
Having some doubt…yet,
Chancing because we never know for sure!

Self-destruction

Destruction comes daily with a morbid mantra
Echoing sounds that resemble death
Two roadblocks and one dead-end
Salutations responses with confused confrontation
The ego long ago bruised and battered
Exhaustion greets and meets the body
While the white flag is rising, surrendering

Tired mind conforms to fatigued physicals
Self-destruction is not an option, but confirmation
The beatings that one has taken are of one's own fault
Dance with the devil, flirt with the devil…
You might as well take on his beliefs

You can't combat because you haven't suited yourself to
     do so
You fall in line with the assembly
Reproducing and manufacturing the negativity that lies
     within
You flirt with sin

Heaven on Earth

No better than this
At present, I am tranquil in this mood
No greater comfort than this now
Death to darkening skies... the sun ascends
No precipitation
Stationed in this calming location
Solemnly in absorption
Solely listening to his beat

Heart rhythms are pacing
Gratitude of this second
Followed by minutes
At last this peaceful hallow
A moment in time anticipated
Heavily awaited
Love's purest form
I have felt heaven on earth

2 a.m.

Something is kind of beautiful
About late night hours
The wind howling
The windows shaking
And all that breeze tapping on the pane

Something is kind of beautiful
About the night
And though I resist rest
As I detest that lay with the bed
I love my peaceful time

Something is quite beautiful
About 2 a.m.
When dreams are featured
And painted in time
I know I love my "me" time

And you know…
As time floats
I resist looking at my watch
Or checking on the clock
Wanting to be frozen in the moment

Something is oh so sweet
And quite unique
About the sounds of this house
The floor squeaks
And the musical droplets in the sink

No dogs barking
No kid's squawking
It's just me and the night
As I resist all fight
Just to face this calming peace

It's beautiful this wee hour
The steaming radiators,
Humming noises,
Wind howling
And I, just typing away at 2 in the morning

A Moment to Remember

If I could reminisce the morning
When the heat turned up
The mood was ever so gentle
His kisses heightened ever peak
When stimulation furled, and curled my toes
Ah because...
It was a moment to remember

If I could reminisce the morning
That dance beneath the sheets
That scurried everything onto the floor
That left me in flames and wanting more
The intensity of his touch...
I would because...
It was a moment to remember

If I could reminisce the morning
That left me tangled in sheets
Feeling a splendid high
With trembles up my thighs
I would lock that memory in forever
Because...
Ah, it was a moment to remember

Heard a Rainbow

Ever hear a rainbow,
I surely would like to try

Would it be a soft soothing melody?
Or a harsh raging sound
Would it whisper lullabies?
Or entrance with me jazz
Would it be that bebop?
Or scattering scats

Composed of cool cat's melodies
Enriched with blaring horns
Deep bass guitar rhythms
Or would it be that big bang
In the big band sound?

Or could it be...
Some rhythm in my blues
I wonder what song it would use

I imagine the rainbow would be music
Perhaps a song
Or would is sound like the love in my Jones
Angelic or could it be
The Congo and jungle mix
Would it supply my gyration fix?
Where my hips and thighs
Get a high
Off bass that demands

Dancing and winding it down
A little Jamaica in its sound

Would it be spicy?
Caliente hot
That makes me do the salsa
The rumba
Or be a little hip in my hop
A rapper's delight
Bars that are tight
Could it have a country twang?
With a little Shania Twain
My rainbow would be a mix of all

I think I did hear the rainbow
Because I dance every time it is around
You should be attentive
For it mimics every sound

Unrecognizable

I don't recognize me,
Not even in the light of the sun
Could I see beyond the distortion

Their lies
Have become
My truth
Their perception,
My mirror

They no longer throw stones
In replacement
Heavier artillery,
Hollow point bullets
Piercing a sunken chest

I wear a toe tag
Nameless
Unknown identity
I remain just a number
In the system

Systematic society
Where birth name
And social code
Is only known

I step among crowds overpopulated
Following the flow

Of feet beating against concrete pavement

Lost…

Buried beneath ashes
Of
The faked death of my mortal self

I live blended
With evil spirits
Gentle, loving, caring and forgiving mask
Now gone

In darkness
You no longer see a falsified persona
The paranoia of company kept
Disturbs my peace
There is an annoyance
Overflowing with intolerance
Again,
I don't recognize me!

Not for Sale

I cannot rot in lowered confidence until it decomposes me
It seems the only thing by my side these days is time
As time fades away, it stales the moment
Dry, brittle, crack feelings in its crumb-like existence
Hoping it will turn into sawdust inside my mind
But as the particles remain, so does remnants of my faith

Spilled milk spoiled,
Crying over wasted emotional goods that have expired...
Not great for a newer display for this assumed commodity
Never wanting to be out of season and in the clearance
department
Sold at a price below my worth
At a cost, less a few cents of a bill

Seems the shelf-life of my self-esteem was not
imperishable
And unbeknownst to me how to preserve it in a jar
The preparation of the presentation of prettied wax paper
and a bow
It did nothing for the sale of intentions
Just distracted you, the window observer from looking at
tampered merchandise
Now hoping to go back to the Manufacturer to become a
better product

The conveyor belt on this assembly line is no good for me
I've been renewed and repackaged and yet there is no other
creation like me

There is no way I can be re-shelved
I am not a buyer's product; there isn't an online auction for
me
My Inventor proud of his repair, displayed me after He
refurbished
Tagged "Not for Sale"
Hoping *WORTH* becomes a billboard and others would
want it

My Sky Seems to Fall

My sky seems to fall
And my earth seems to climb
When there is sadness
I am caught between the lines

There is sorrow I cannot control
And bitterness within my heart
There is darkness in my soul
I seem to be falling apart

And if you ever thought you know
Then you are just as blind
See my sky seems to fall
As my earth seems to climb

My inner-verse has corrosion
There seems to be droughts of rain
The atmosphere is quite dry
And the air is full of pain

It hurts to breathe again
The normalcy of inhaling and to exhale
My skin feels colder now
Lack of color, I'm quite pale

I tapped into my instincts
Where intellect greets the spirit nudging
Only Faith and common sense…
Will keep me from grudging

To refrain from the tale of hurt
Or the agony of defeat
As you see my sky seems to fall
As my earth seems out of reach

My Scars

Illustrated within lines on my wrist
My external scars of mental anguish
And even if I have internally healed
My secret, my past, my pain revealed

On my forearm are jagged blade lines
The scars are visual and still fresh in the mind
Once carved with the intent to kill;
After my stomach, wouldn't stomach the pills

At fifteen and now twenty-two years later
A reminder when I told myself "I hate her"
Incisions in plain view for all to see…
Do not make me regret one part of me!

I do not try to hide what my past holds
Time and time again, the story retold
Image of disgust on another's face
They follow with their eyes each line they trace

The scars are there in plain view
A constant reminder of what I went through
But also, a reminder that I am blessed to be alive
The life I once had, and the life I revived

Illustrated within the lines on my wrist
My externals scars of mental anguish
And even if I had internally healed
My secret, my past, my pain revealed

Dear Sweet Darling:

Sweet beautiful darling:

With eyes, true likeness of mother's pain
Your tears cascading…

And I have no answers as to why.
"Why does Mommy cry?"

I try to barricade you inside my arms,
Keep you sheltered from other's harm
There is nothing in this entire world
Beyond the earth's atmosphere,
The universe...
And the heavens that I wouldn't do for you

Your courage and innocence of great wisdom… has me
amazed
Each day I tell you how beautiful you are
How smart you are and what lovely personality you have
You're witty and funny and tickle me pink the way you
make me laugh

"Why does Mommy cry?"

Mommy is going through a phase

"What is a phase?"

But no reply you get from me

Mommy doesn't want to lie, you see
And Webster's version may not register to you:
Any of the major appearances or aspects in which a thing
of varying modes or conditions manifests itself to the eye or
mind.

…But what Mommy wants to say

The mold of my heart has been broken, my mind unfocused
and dwelling. I am part-cold but you keep me warm. I am
saddened and beset by pain… agony… regret… Oh, how I
wish I could soon forget. I just need rest… To rest this
restless mind,

and peace…

I need harmony within myself. I need the strength of the
brick house that not even the Big Bad Wolf could huff and
puff down. I need to withstand the wind, from the big bad
breath of the monsters that attack body, mind, and soul.

I just want to keep the demons away from you
Praying to the Almighty he sees you through
And when I am down I hear you
"I love you"
The sweetest sound ears have ever heard…
Those three words from my darling you,
Has helped your mother pull herself through

I don't know how to explain to an eight-year-old my fears
I just know I don't want you to see my tears
And I don't want to see your cries because I held in mine
Because you feel what's held internal
It reflects in the likeness of your own
Just because you are a part of me
And I, you…
So please do not weep
Please don't feel bad, because Mommy is sad
It has nothing to do with you
My sweet beautiful darling

Butterfly Kisses

Jarred butterfly kisses released,
Freedom warrants such beauty within the air.

Unconfined silken wings tizzy to teach the sky of modest
love.

Never chase it, to recapture it…
Or you'll watch as she flaps her wings to escape!
You must not smother this butterfly, nor take away her
freedom.

Choose her carefully
And please allow the butterfly to select you as well.
The stunning array of her garden, there is one destined for
you.

From a distance,
Admire her spawning allure with a visual eye.

Learn to appreciate this butterfly's colorful exquisiteness
from afar.
And be patient…

Watch her flight to you as the doves.
Simply acknowledge her presence…
Or

Just let her be…
That beautiful butterfly will return her kisses to thee.

Lonely Blues ~ Part II

Keeping to oneself, purposely
Without purposeful intentions
Draws a yearning knocking
Waiting to get into the doors of a vacant heart

And if one is willing
To open the door to a guarded place
Removing the locks and chains
They open themselves to possibilities

Part of this task is to expose oneself with risks
Preparation of letting go of fear
Must be in it, to get anything out of it
And if you refused, you've missed opportunities

Accusations that flutters irregular heartbeats
Chest congestion, failures of the heart
Tired and wearied ways leave a sign on the door
Keep Out!

To want the allowance of letting someone close
But I am to my own demise
Lonelier than before as my blues sing,
Soulful messages of desperation

Calling out his name, but he doesn't exist
I've managed to imagine him as much as I imagined love
Lonely blues soundtracks the soulful yearnings
Desire is calling… ignoring is easy

Time and time again, I can talk my way out of it
Going numb to resist the pain
Paining because I've chosen love
Not allowing love to choose me

Years of solitude, no human connection
No desires to display human affection
Retreating to a lonelier place
Remaining hostage to my fears

5 a.m.

Sorrows of yesterday are erased with the promising of the
rising sun.
How former times were filled with things I did, but cannot
be undone…

At this hour, I resist the sensation to feel…
This lonely existence I continue to live.

Reflections…
I think of you.
Missing you,
Wishing I was brave enough to love you.
And wishing you had the courage to demand it from me.

5 a.m.
I listen…
No birds chirp…
The air still,
My cup half-filled
Coffee is my only comfort now!!!

They race, my thoughts…
Every which way to you!
Avoidance…
I won't let them focus on just one thing.
Figured if I reflect too long, that I will neglect my ability to
avoid!

Sweat…

Any thought of it,
Directs itself to you…
That self-clinging t-shirt filled with your masculine scent
that hugged your body image perfectly…
Sweat…
Ooo… how it leads to our beginning and ending… our one
embrace!

There are things in life we try not to regret…
And there are things held within our memory, which we
will never forget…
Wow…
Your sweat!!!

I surely believe that you bathe in cocoa butter daily,
How else could your coverage be so flawless…?
That your skin…
Has become such a butterscotch sin!!!

5 a.m.
My thoughts of sweet candied coated you…
Dissolves on my palette…
Only leaves a tart remain

Sorrows of yesterday are erased with the promising of the
rising sun.
How former times were filled with things I did, but cannot
be undone…

At this hour, I resist the sensation to feel…
This lonely existence I continue to live.

Reflections…
I think of you.
Missing you,
Wishing I was brave enough to love you.

Love Visage

The heart can distract the mind
Bring turmoil or confusion or elation and jubilation
I find myself in all while in love

One may dispute what another heart may feel
Yet there is only one voice, one set tone to that rhythm

Some are bold enough to say that love has a mind of its
own
It plays by its own rules
Sometimes it can disassociate you from reality
Cause while you are in that moment
Basking in its heavenly glow
You may become unaware of the storm outside the window

It takes a certain kind of courage to listen
Adjusted ears find meaningful songs in love's humming
It's more than a fine-tuned harmony
It defines more than a melody that syncs and modifies
tempos
More than the vibrated low pitch symphony
Unique compositions are splendid while suspended in
warped tones
I guess that is why you can feel the love in music
Cause love is music on its own

Love strives,
It pushes you beyond what you are
Remodels, reconstructs, rebuilds and strengthens structure

It cannot be measured, weighted or sized
Yes, love is heavy

Also, deep, in the way that it is profound and bottomless
Mysterious… ah yes, mysterious it is
Very cryptic and enigmatic
And it is magic
You run out of words once trying to define
You can't describe, summarize or explain
It just is…

And what it is can be different for each of us

My love is in the senses,
Touch, taste, smell, sight, and hearing
Each and every one is heightened and over-stimulated
Love is a palpable dessert, sweet…very
Soft, like a cloud of cotton balls on the tenderness of spots
To say, love, smell like a rose would be offensive
And yet, it is not that poetic for me…
Love is in the pouring of his pores… sweat, has that affect
And I swear I can't see love, I am so blinded by it…
Love is spirited
And last, can you hear it
Love sound waves ripples through hearts, jump starts
Restarts and still can be the same lyrics, different song

Don't Want to Be Sober

With all this love for my man, it becomes intoxicating
I come to be a bit tipsy
And a little dizzy in love
He got me tripping over my feet
Clumsy in his gigantic smile and mesmerizing presence
Got me stumbling over here in his real love essence

I feel the butterflies in my belly
My knees weak, my legs like jelly
And when he comes close
Giving me a dose
Of his whew... lip lock--- I melt
Because his soul is felt
Intertwining and combining emotional concoctions of
intense passion
Telling him this kind of consumption needs to be rationed

While under the influence in his addictive flames
And tongued tied on his name...
I feel flutters
This waving sensation in my tummy
Got me flip-flopping and diving in the ocean of wino love
Riding out these ripples
Adoring the currents because that is the way love flows
And I tell you, each night my desire grows

I am so caught up inside his heavy gin & tonic, bionic
motions
His lovemaking is 180 proofs

Immobile off his bourbon elixir tangling-of-the-sheets fun
Stupor from liquored passion rum
I am way past lit from his Willie Wonka vodka
He is the intoxicant my body needs
And I am sorry, but no meetings are necessary

While boozed-up in his firm and concentrated hold,
I completely malfunction and he has all control
He is my melody and here I am humming his songs of
adoration
I am a lush for his tenderness, there is no moderation

My self-discipline when in his company is nonexistent
Because his soft touch can bring on tingles
And have me hammered into a zone
Sending mental and physical vibrations
That can last all night long
Inside potent heated fluctuations... directed to my nerve
sensations
Transporting chills and again... intoxication

I am inebriated from his love
A drunken monkey that just can't get enough of... it
And I don't ever want to be sober

The Skeleton Key to My Closet

They have been buried long enough... memories
Blurred into a forgetful place inside my mind,
I wish not to tackle them now,
Nor do I want to bring forth the pain
I do not want to remember

They have happened... dreadful things
If I do not speak of, I can leave the dust settled
For the cobwebs, I do not wish to clean
I wish for the memories to rot in time,
Yet instead they seem to rot my mind

Skeletal remnants remain in my closet
A reminder, a stench of funk in my blues
As I wish my secrets to fade within aging,
They become vintage horrors
Although not of this time, still of relevance

I want my bad memories to wane
Not to be restored and showcased for all to see
Not to reveal my vulnerability inside my human qualities
But I cannot be unstuck, myself until I deal with it
With what is locked inside my closet

On my necklace the key I removed,
Opening as I access my inner closet
Worn and brittle issues come falling out
It doesn't seem to carry the worth it use to
Back then it seemed to almost cost me my life

The skeleton key to my closet seems useless now,
I can discard and clean everything
Nothing to hold me bound here, no more vintage horrors,
No more fears of the revealed,
And at last, no more holding place

Crushin'

Heightened vocally,
your tone sounds off in waves
Sending rifts inside my tummy,
Experiencing a feel, I never felt before
Giving me something to think about
Something to explore

My moistened thighs,
gets a rise off tender imaginings...
I think you deserve a pair of wings,
the way you take me higher within my dreams
We got a groovy kind of attraction,
mind boggled over the reaction
How I get clumsy
and fall all into you

Now it's all baby talk,
with the goo-goo and googled eyes
and the beginner steps...
I get lost in that vibe
until we become chill...

Less deepened conversation...
we take a breather, come up for air
giggling and making small gibberish
sideline jokes while juggling feelings
I'm talking schoolyard crushes
and cherry red blushes...
cuz we cool like dat

The Lost (as explained to me)

Options become limitless as we reinvent, reconstruct,
reprogram, and redirect our minds.
Some of us are "lost" and we like it…

The quest becomes a way of living,
an antidote to those who feel purposeless.
Striving to find the owner of the soul who eyes stares back
in the reflective looking glass is as daring as bungee diving
off a cliff.
The excitement, the adrenaline pusher, the metabolic sensor
of hiking into overdrive…

Deep breaths, inhale and exhaling gases of change…
The lost…symbolic of being deranged…
what's even stranger…
is that we are more in tune with ourselves
than most will ever be.

We do not plant our feet in soils of deceit…
We are constantly on the hunt; in truth, we seek…
We are the global mystique
Looked upon as being one of the weak,
While others vacation, or escaping by using drugs or
medication… to find inner peace;
we comfort ourselves inside our mind, this is our retreat.

We are the explorers; we compass off instinct.
We are seen as the doubtful, the terrors of being torn…
Yet we are the believers of transformation, of being reborn

We can't secure ourselves in this body,
nor be bound by a clock.
Time is fed to us in teaspoons, the anti-aging we are.

We pace ourselves in stages; our wisdom count is our ages.
We study; we enhance; we develop; enriching our lives by
never feeling grounded.
The lost…
Pursuits are commenced, hoping never to be found.

Bound by the ties of revelations and epiphanies, there are
ideas and thought processes to be rediscovered.
For the lost has been branded wrong with a scarlet letter.
The founders, the initiators; we are the creators of how to
find inner peace…
We are the authors of philosophies; we are the stargazers,
also, the road pavers, who have concreted roads to self-
discovery…

You pity us… the lost,
we are not misplaced… our sanction is within our
scrimmaging.
We are the pioneers of the mind, going deeper into the
realms of where no man has dared to go before.
Yes, we are the explorers…
the real paranormal activity.

The lost,

the intentional, whose attention is geared toward thought action,
our satisfaction is slighter greater than none.
The myth of being disconnected is as false as the cliché the sky is the limit.
If there ever was a limit, believe me; we've already gone beyond it.

Energetic within our focus… our visions are of self-inquiry and of our own personal truths.
Once reaching a threshold of purpose, we purposed higher, ignited are our appetite's fires…
Our desire is to erase the circle of thoughts. Redefine the lines of a squared thinker.
And challenge the concept of infinity…

No…, we do not call ourselves GOD, we call upon divinity.

Probably we are closer to spirituality than one found could ever be.
Relations with the Almighty are a necessity, whoever that might be,
because it differs for every one of us.

Only to you, we are lost, but you are the one stuck in a box.

Penetrating deeper into the unknown, we roam.
In dark and enlightened places… we roam!

Unreached territories, yes, we roam.
We are not thirsting creatures as portrayed,
no, we are not the insane or enslaved to our own brain.

You have scarlet us "lost" and we have been betrayed.
We are the forefathers that have paved the way…
The pacesetters and the explorers to the inner-world,
We are the achievers of understanding and the miners of
knowledge.
We drill deeper beyond the surfaced perceptions.
Pilgrimaging beyond the basic questions of who, what,
when, where and why's.

We are legends in our own right,
when our bodies finally meet the earth's dust, our thoughts
rise and never dies.

I SEE LOVE

Draping my thoughts,
You pulled the curtain over my eyes
Shaded them in obscured affection
Then to illustrate adoration's resurrection,
All that I could see,
Was LOVE!

Covered in thick smog
This land of everlasting
This world of reveries of endless pleasures;
The film pulled back and drew
And all that I could see,
Was you!

Stars lit once blue now black inked skies,
The moon lying lazily within the dusk
Dawn's yawning, impatient for her return
Becomes radiant, while flirts with lively hues creating an imprint
All that I could see,
Was the Sun!

Shadows uncovered to expose beautiful faces,
I notice an inspiring twinkle within your eyes
Trueness of soul reveals an untold history
Optic illusions disappeared, dissolving the mystery;
There before me... all I could see,
Was this LOVE!

The Beauty of a Woman

The exquisiteness of a woman buds like a delicacy
She is a pictorial of grace
Visually tempting optical bouquet
But not to be shelved or left on display

Her allure is in her soulful foundation
Admirers can't help but get a whiff
A hint of her sensual and noble scent
Both beauty and strength they represent

Entrenched in her beliefs
Her roots stand resilient although petite
She is a warrior in her own right

Her growth comes from God's light
She blossoms with His wisdom
And blessed is she
Behold with your eyes a rose for all to see

I Was Supposed to Feed Her

I failed...
I failed her when I failed me...
Because I was supposed to feed her, not bleed her into
reality

She's that seed, that needs to believe... so she can grow an
inch
But my funky stench, don' spoiled her

I might have shattered a dream, while I forgot how to
Not providing or giving her something to strive to....
Guess I don' lied too...
I mean not revealing is just like stealing...
Robbing her of truth!

I feel that if I don't water her,
Quench that thirst inside of her... it's just like misleading
her...
I guess what I prefer,
Is to just say exactly what it is, how it is...
and maybe it's none of her biz to know...
Maybe it's the experience she needs to grow

But why would I want her to experience my math,
Taking an uneducated guess and walking down my narrow
path...
I need her to see, that she ain't me... although a part of me
That my flaws can teach her not to reach a blur

How not to fantasize fur... when the temperature's hot in a
cold cold world
Show her how not to become frozen in this insanity...
I mean can you really blame me?

So, I guess I didn't pass... my parenting class...
Cuz, I'm at a blank when it comes to her...
Just cuz I don't dream doesn't mean to interrupt hers...
Maybe she'll just so happen to like diamond and furs...
Not because of false representation of meaning
Not because of a status of being...
Maybe it'll just be something she prefers...
Perhaps it could be a part of a motivation to stir her...

But I can't live a life on suppose and maybe's
I'm damn near forty but lived life like I'm eighty...
I've experienced the most bitter of what life can give...
And that's for damn sure not the life I want her to live

So...
I failed...
I failed her when I failed me
I was supposed to feed her, not bleed her into reality...
but yet she remains with innocent eyes...
That's well aware of the danger that lurks outside

And nothing is wrong being outside of a bubble,
I mean, heck...

There is fresh air, a relaxing breeze... the feel of softness,
yet not naïve...
Knowing that out there sets other's dirt... ready to
contaminate, and seek to hurt...
I guess all in all she doesn't mind... in hopes to find... that
if I just allow it...
I might just see... that I'm more of her than she is of me...

Maybe she's here to teach...

Maybe her purpose is to reach... to show me
That I'm not always facing oblivion...
Perhaps inside, like her... maybe...
Maybe,
I too, need to dream!

Love Out Loud!

When love is held beneath the breath
It smothers itself within hesitation

LOVE OUT LOUD

Let it be heard
Let it be known

Love so vivid, even the blind shall see
Love that conquers... seizes over the negativity
Love that converts, changes its form within its growth
Love that discerns...
I'm talking love that teaches and love that learns
Love that is audible, even to deafen ears
And love that does not reduce itself to the unseen
Love that knows no fears

LOVE OUT LOUD

Let it be heard
Let it be known

Love with no worries, love with no concerns
Love that enriches itself beyond the fleshly yearns
Love's light so luminous, it reveals, it shows
Love that is not of ignorance,
Because it simply knows

Let love be a bridge,

Crossing you over to the other side
Love that is not selfish and love that obliges

LOVE OUT LOUD

Let it be heard
Let it be known
Never keep it hidden
Let it be shown

Love that produces peace
And peace within you to care
Love, that will make you take
And the love that makes you share
Love that makes you restraint...
And the love that makes you dare

Love so vivid, even the blind shall see
Love that conquers... seizes over the negativity
Love that listens with an open ear
Love which fathoms
Love which wisdoms
Pure love...
True love...
Real love...
Love that fills
Love seeping outside
Released from pores
Love that creates the sexiest amour

Physical love
Mental love
Emotional love
Spiritual love... Agape

LOVE OUT LOUD...

Let it be known
Let it be shown
Let love be!

Internal Vision

his eyes ran through me
discovering the fullness of my heart
emptying me with his internal vision
he meticulously roamed my fantasies
the intrusion of my private yearnings
he saw beyond this skinned structure
straight into the depth of my secret self
sampling me with a studied focus

his eyes wandered thoroughly
discovering the deeper me
his probing intensified as he infringed my space
removing all mystery with a knowing stare
admiring through the windows of my soul
seeing me unmade and flawed
his eyes ran through me
and he loves me still

Intrusion

His words intrude upon
My consciousness
Plagues me like a bad habit,
That I have not formed
The mentality to give up

It lingers long within my thoughts
Taking hostage
Over my mind

I find myself engulfed into chaos
The struggle is no longer with self
But with my logic and interpretation
Of events, past and present
It frustrates me,
Depletes me of all energy
Just to give the processing of
These occurrences

I've had it up to here---
No more playing the victim
Nor will I become receptive of bullshit
I finalized the woe is me method
And I've even traveled
Down the forget the world path
Who needs love lane
And I-hate-you boulevard
All roads lead to a destructive dead end

No one can get close enough
To transfer the negativity of this
Unbalanced and disturbed universe
I have no one to blame but myself really

I have adapted a do or die recipe for life
Adjusted the seasoning
To create the best gourmet existence
Life as I know it has changed
Has become quite strange
And somewhat deranged
Yet… and even still,
I have learned to maintain

Though at times I may not appear
To be well balanced
Thrown off my axis
But still stubborn enough
To know
That I cannot conform, will not conform

And no matter what words
Intrude upon my consciousness
I have learned to resist
The chaotic bearings
But if nothing positive goes in
And negativity seeps through
Pores on skin,
I begin to wear its funky fragrance

More bees draw near
To the sweetness of honey
And the Assholes,
Find familiar of such funk
They swarm around as if
They found their home

I have found comfort
In being alone
And as his thoughts intrudes
It's my best-formed method
Of ignoring their deceit
Is to build a wall
Of reinforced concrete
With steel bars
And explosives at entrance
Ready and willing to destroy
Anyone who declares to intrude

Me, Myself and I

In the midst of my muddled surroundings,
I made time for ME today
Reintroducing Me and Myself to I
A dialogue of inspiration and motivation became indecisive
Me and Myself disagreed, as I stayed in the middle
Quarreling to whom to position first

The acceptable conclusion conceived…
A bonding of three would become impossible to conquer
That the LOVE inside this circle could not be shaken or
stirred
Together,
A vision would be born,
And collectively their thoughts shall be heard

Whether it would be in the open or discrete,
These ladies shall meet
To uphold a purpose
Studying their book of guidance
As they seek counseling
To maintain this sacred bond

Sweet meditation…
To soothe their soul, as a whole
Destined to feel complete,
They met…
Touched and kneeled,
In prayer

Save her! Prayed Me, for Myself
Give her Peace, asked I, for Me
May she feel whole, Myself requested for I
And in their circle, they rejoiced and cried,
Promising to God together they will stand, never to divide,
In unison, they spoke… "Thank you, Lord"!

Not a Pessimist

No falsehoods of ideas for change
I cannot feed myself bull for fuel
No deceitful pledges of promises
That I cannot keep
Refusal to read lying lips
That is from my own self-indulging practice
No longer coaching myself
I know better!
No more fabricated ideas
To keep me accompanied at night
Wiping the slate clean
While I purposely forgot to dream
Scratching off other's expectations,
With my sharpie
I have learned to live
With eyes, wide open

Avoidance

All my life I've been living in avoidance
Trying to curb the difficult feelings that are stirring inside
Evading the situational cues that trigger the pain
Blanking my mind to anti-revel the memories
I've built bridges that I've purposely demolished
Leaving me all by my lonesome
Feeling accomplished in my dissociation with the torment
Knowing that anguish would greet me again on the other
side

My denial was not the end to the pain
That learned numbness would not be the freeing agent
I sought it to be
Unbeknownst to me, it would cause further damage
Adding weight to the pain I carried, causing more suffering
It created fresher wounds to old scars
Producing newer scabs and infections to something
appearing healed

Avoidance... it held me back from living
It took away definition to life's meaning
I was in zombie mode going through the motions
and not feeling
Removal of daily pleasures in my life... I was no longer
enjoying fresh air
I could not see the beauty in God's nature
Focusing on PAIN...
pain alone, dissecting it and reviving it
Smothering myself inside of it... I couldn't breathe!

It was no longer about people's judgment
I've taken over and was harsher than any other could be
The formation of self-blaming and self-bashing began
My thoughts took over and initiated a life of its own
I was spellbound by my inner nature's destructive hold
I fed myself this poison and it became my beliefs

But...

I could no longer run, no longer hide, no longer escape
Soul searching and re-evaluation was inevitable
I had to reconnect myself to feeling
Touching the base discovering the core to my suffering
I've prayed... many times I have kneeled
And yet my prayers were empty,
Eventually, I learned that I must feel it, to let it go...
Acknowledging it to set it free
Ignoring doesn't make it go away... sometimes just
embellishes it later

I learned to be kind to my pain
Stroke it, touch it gently and treat it with light
My experience with it was not like before
I gave it the worth it deserved...
took from it what I could learn
Then I released it into the wild...
let it go from whence it came
Freeing it... to free me

Avoidance,
It is not preventative
In life, we are not defending ourselves by blocking issues
To resolve one must solve
Do yourself a merit of justice...
Feel it, learn from it, and let go!

Heels

So, you wanted to wear my shoes
But I have both good and bad news
They were new when I bought them
With you in them, they are slightly used

Visions of wearing my clogs is what you had
But they are still mine, so now you're sad
Looked at the purse that matched to the tee
But you can't wear what was meant for me

You wanted to take a walk in my shoes
Fit for size, before you choose
You thought you'd get in my heels, without having to pay
But you got heartache and pain, at the end of the day

Thought you had a connection with those heels
Would take them over, and try to steal
Thought you'd slip on the pumps I wear
And took a walk, so you dared

But you fell, and since have not gotten up
In a tight position, now you're stuck
Shouldn't be wearing anyone else's stilettos
Tried to look like a lady, but came across as a hobo

I told you to stay away from my house and home
Yet you were bold enough to go into my closet and roam
You had the nerves to try on my boots and heels
You wanted to be me, so how does it feel?

Coveting your neighbor's shoes
Now you're feeling quite used and abused
Yet, even still… you're longing to step back into my heels
Getting lost in your illusion of what's unreal

Trying on my expensive footwear
But they belong to me, you didn't care
Thought I wouldn't notice that you tried them on
Wanting what I have just to intrude upon

Wow no remorse and the shoes didn't fit
The pair you wanted, you did not get
You bravely invaded my heels at any cost
Now you are shoeless and very lost

You tried to break the stitch and sole
To ruin them completely was your goal
One day I hope that you just try being you
Because my heels are MINE, and they still wear like new

Unwoven Tapestry

They become unlaced and unwoven,
Into threads of forgotten strings
No longer knotted,
They hang separately
Each now unique and distinguished
The ending of a once sturdy tapestry

Symbolic of each man and every woman
Standing alone, unbothered
Segregated and isolated by self-idealism
As each of their importance outweighs
The other until it eliminates
No longer complementary
But a hazard marked in red flags

It seemed unions turned into business deals,
Lacking the spiritual and moral fibers
That once sealed matrimony in vows of
Til death do us part
What happened to for sickness and in health
Or that one about for richer or poorer
It must have got lost in promiscuity and
In no life matters…
Because a five minute lay in the hay
Will reproduce the self-hate that it takes
To bring into the world another you
Just to walk away

No solidarity continued unwinding strands

Grandma does what she can do,
But it is so out of her hands
So many fatherless children,
So many mothers gone wild
No security within the home…
Wondering why the streets raised their child

Our GOD left the schools
Our bloodshed makes the news
And more and more…
We've become unlaced and unwoven,
Into threads of forgotten strings
No longer knotted,
They all hang separately
Each now unique and distinguished
The ending of a once sturdy tapestry

Sex Sells

Sex sells like the open line for souls
Luscious bods reap the growths…
Of men genitals that lust for those
Who body maximized the infatuation

Depicted in photos she posts online without hesitation
The new generation
Where to indulge into mind stimulation… first
Could be worse… no one wants to feel these days

We'll just shut off our minds,
And share our bodies…
So, that's the trend…
I suppose!

But wow!!!... Look how she's posed!!!

At her… the women turn up their nose
All the while the men fantasize and label her sensual…
Is that how it goes???
I suppose!!!

Sex sells,
An erotic spell…
Of lustful thinking… caught and sinking into a persona!

Do you wanna… wanna!!!
The men ask without blinking twice
Even though at home he as a wife,

But wow!!! … She looks nice!!!
Is that, right?
Hell, No!!!...
But sex sells!

I Said NO!

A soft touch
turned into the blades of a thousand knives
a bleak perception
widened my opened eyes
drainage of tears fell in a dripping faucet motion
reflections of a nightmare
was my living reality

A pleasing touch
oh, how my body responded
the teasing of temptation
and trusting… everything he supposedly stood for

I was the passion in his eyes
or was that lust?
I could not distinguish from the two…
until resistance grew powerful
and his strength out strengthen mine

I knew that a struggle was coming on
my hands grasped at my button
and his,
easily pulled it apart
I couldn't hold them together
and yet still could not distinguish play from assault

He gave up (so I thought)

Entranced by such softness… tenderness

abruptly stunned by a yank
a yank that obliterated all pleasure
the REALITY, that yes… this is a struggle

My pants half past down my hips
I fought to flip over, a tug-a-war with my bottoms, trying to
keep them up
yanking...
he kept tugging at them, pulling them down
and down they fell…
He forced my legs to open wide... left me exposed
with his heavyweight, he laid on top of me

I said NO!
first in my mind
and then sternly with my mouth

There was an insertion… his penetration
(I think God removed me from my body)

The thing was,
it was as if my body was calling this creep

Granted,
no creep was he when I was in awe of this man,
when I was intrigued, and minutes before desired his touch
but what he wanted was way too much
much more than what I was willing to give

(Here I am in defensive mode)

Regardless of the situation,
I said NO!

Wet was my flesh, and though my body was inviting…
my mouth again said "NO!"

"Get off me"
"Kiss me and I'll get off," he said.
"GET OFF ME!"
"Kiss me and I'll get off."
It took everything out of me, my lips brushed his cheek
"No, kiss me like you mean it", I heard him say
"Kiss me like before"

I almost died!
BEFORE, I thought...

Yes, before…, I wanted this man
that I first liked
then wasn't sure
and then I loathed for his disregard,
his obtrusive force
and now sexual abuse,
just wanting him to GET OFF OF ME!

I didn't want to know how I felt against his flesh

nor hear his commentating on what pleasure he was receiving
what rise he was feeling
as he violated my body
I didn't want him lying there… on top of me
As he ignored my pleas for him to STOP

Was he insane?
better yet was I?
how could I have let this happen?

I said "NO"!
I said "NO"!

(Rape is a crime of violence and domination in which one person forces, coerces, or manipulates another person into sexual intercourse. Date Rape occurs when there is forced or coerced sex within a dating relationship. With Acquaintance Rape, the act is committed by someone known to the victim. Nearly 2/3 of all victims between the ages of 18 and 29 reported that they had a prior relationship with their attacker.)

She Didn't Know How to Make Love

She could not fulfill his loving desires
Because she knew not how to make love
Conflicted in her mind what sex was
Sex to her was a selfish act of perversion that men forced
upon women
And sadly, to little girls
It had no tender meaning attached

She could not make love to her husband
Although loving him more than her
but his penetration triggered horrific memories
Deeper inside her warm and inviting thighs was her secret
She felt violated although every thrust was immeasurable
pleasure

Sex would be the way she revealed aggression
Clitoris sensations had physical stimulation
But mentally every gyration and hip roll had taken its toll
Conflicted...

Fucking would be the way she tortured herself
She knew that yes, he was receiving sexual gratification
But the movement within her demonstration spelled
H-A-T-E
Something she could not verbally communicate
She would use her own body as a weapon against herself
Because on the inside she was oh so numb and empty

She knew not how to display affection

He would hold her closely at night and feel her repulsion
She would tremble, shake as her frame went into
convulsions
Oh, he loved her so, but her secrets he did not know

So many sexual violations and the raping of her spirit
She grew to despise everything about herself
If someone said she was pretty she thought, it was a curse
They were only being nice, but it felt something worse
Any compliment about her looks felt like an assault

Alternating the size of her bodily structure
To protect, she purposely gained weight
While under major stress she would deteriorate
Up and down on the scale was another drastic measure of
self-hate

Her existence she loathed
How many mirrors would she break because of a distorted
truth in her reflection?
Why didn't she know that she was God's perfection?

She didn't know how to make love
Because she had no love for the woman she was

Eventually, love came with a price of sacrifice
She would learn to unlock the doors of her closet
Let loose of all the skeletal remnants

She confided in the man that chose to love her despite her
issues

She didn't know how to make love
But a new-found love for herself would free her
A woman in peace would be her
And a man who now understood his wife,
Could teach her

Soldier Down

Wounded by the very ones we care for
The hurt goes beyond an ache in the bones
Internal damages in slowly to heal places
Maybe it's something time can fix

A nasty sting to the heart, it kills character
Especially if not treated right away
The venom is pumping through veins
Extremely tired is the mind
The heart weeps for its last beat
Skin becomes scaly, the poison travels faster
Another toxin is used as a choice antidote to numb
Damages take its wages
"Soldier down"

One's bravery and ability to once hold things in order
Finds itself in array, it's their clutter he faced
Can't seem to identify himself without his dog tag
Who's left to pick up the pieces?

All that is left is a war zone…
It now seems deserted, abandoned… and a hopeless place
"Soldier down"

Wounded by his peers
His artillery is less effective…
His armor wasn't meant for use against the trusted

Their methods to destroy was underhanded

To use his own mind against him
To damage him in places where vulnerability would seep in
Their plot and ploy would be evil!

But you can't conquer God's soldier…

No weapon formed against him shall prosper
When his faith wavered,
They wanted to completely unarm him…

A soldier of love…
They wanted to harm him…

His light… so bright
He was blinded by his frienemies...
But... their betrayal failed!!!
Their best manipulation… also Failed!!!!

"Soldier stands"

Sometimes you can get a good man down…
And yet, a man of God won't stay there for long!

Poetic Affair

a love affair begins
with words and music
the collaboration of a poetic muse
the birth of a melodic concoction
forms a brew of passion
a love dance is inspired
songs of the soul transpired
and the bass is pumping…
heartbeats

Grown Folks

I remember when I was younger,
The elders smoked their Kools and played the blues
While sitting at the table
Lights low, the music flow
And a cuss word here and there
It was a grown-up affair,
The cards laid across the table
And the glasses half filled with ice
And the mood was nice
As the music sufficed
And a couple or two slow danced in the middle of the floor
Had me adore
The way they moved
The way they grooved
And the smooth attitude
As the night elude
Loving the grown folks and what they do

Love in Darkness

I became visionless when it came to love
my eyes would not let me see its blithe
I evolved into a sanction of bleakness
the road of traveled love... lost

It was love in darkness

My sensitivity hardens
my luminous glow dimmed
only sadness sparkled from these eyes

Sorrowful and misunderstood

Love me, love me not
either way, your fog will clear
and assumptions will be no more
the day will arrive,
the definition will soon have meaning
and the shadows of my emotions
shall no longer be shaded by defensiveness

Submissive to my longings
purging from discomfort

It was love in darkness

How can I bring to the light
what once use to be,
the irrelevancy of it now

The past cannot be erased
the future scripted by our desires
and willfulness to change things

Say no more of yesterday, of last night...
I pray that today will have substance
and that I will see the likes of virtue in you

See me, as I see you,
as we proclaim something new beyond the stars
you are shining on my crystal heart
that I may love again,
outside of the darkness

Magnified Love

Under transparency and microscopic viewing,
by far illusive, what was seen with naked eye
was magnified
and dignified
it became a distinguished love

The kind you wish and dream of
the exact kind dreams are made of
I witnessed in you

Beneath the shadowing reflective
all sparkly
and presence of new
it was you
and your love under the glass

In an array of a gorgeous display
Even with a sunken spirit
I still had to get near it
To see the blemish
I knew God was not finished
With His art of a complete man

I understand how we sometimes fall
to rise tall… again
with all that I see beneath the glass
Beyond the stunning display

Seems a spirit that needed restoration

Without hesitation
or complete evaluation
I wanted what was under the glass

Love that lasts

My heart was right under the glass with you
and within that moment…
I was too

Dying

It was almost like tip-toeing among the clouds
That eternal dreaming fog-like feeling
It was a moment of seeing faces,
Then seeing none at all
I was no longer of this earth

It was almost like heavenly hymns whispering
Softened melodies crept inside a stilled cadenced heartbeat
Pulses generated and rhythms returned
Light in every symbolism was seen
Eyelids finally opened

It was almost like a phenomenon,
And yet I greatly describe it as a miracle from GOD
No words of importance can depict dying,
When being alive to tell...
It is a blessing to be here

The Thunder in My Tears

This morning I cried,
Last night I cried...
Yesterday afternoon and evening...
I cried!
Though I said nothing was wrong...
I lied...
Attempting to get over it...
I tried!

Pouring out tear after tear
Clutching my chest,
A heart full of fears
Breaking while dissipating
Slowly wasting... in this
Organic funk...

Scattered across the floor
One by one...
Journal after another,
Page after page
The same monotonous
Coding of my melancholy in black ink
Into self,
I sink
Mind blank...
Can't think
Just concentrated on the hues
Looking for the right color to paint my blues

Down in the dumps,
Feeling a bit recycled
Complete in my blankness...
A bit confused
Not one of you/ not one of you...
Have been in my shoes
Now you want to talk,
But leave your judgment
Before your words
You choose

This morning I cried,
Last night I cried...
Yesterday afternoon and evening...
I cried!
Though I said nothing was wrong...
I lied...
Attempting to get over it...
I tried!

I've seen stormy days
And insecurity in my ways
This mask I wear is not for display
It's to hide the words...
I wish not to say
In sadness, I lay
As I tend to stray
Into a zone of the forbidden
There is thunder in my tears...

And no, I'm not kidding

I hide before the lightning strikes
I can feel the rumble in my brain
Blatantly I am a murderer of self
Many times, I have been slain

My weeping reverberates,
There is a chill within my song
I belt the lyrics of my pain
And to the too excruciating,
I hum along

In this world of righteousness
I feel that I am wrong
& upon this earth where life is,
I feel I don't belong

So, I am alone...

This morning I cried,
Last night I cried...
Yesterday afternoon and evening...
I cried!
Though I said nothing was wrong...
I lied...
Attempting to get over it...
I tried!

The thunder in my tears
Is filled with all that I am feeling
Just existing in this world
In this life that I should be living
Don't know how to take
I am giving... giving... giving
Giving enough until I break
Then in my mind,
I am reliving, reliving, reliving
All the pain and torment

I long to let it go
My misery doesn't like company,
I learn to let you go
I let go
I let go...
I let... go
You never understood the process
So, you never turned away
I did a reverse
And you asked me to meet you half way

I trembled when I cried
I heard the roar when I wept
My body shook violently
As you held me as I slept
The thunder in my tears
The most vicious release
Carried on within my dreams

Not one moment of peace

The cycle begins again...
This morning...
I cried!

Stranger Within My Mind

Every day there seems to be a search to find myself
Feeling absent in this cypher of life
Answers are revealed and I seem to question
My mind plays tricks on me in that instance
Where I just need to be in the know

How can I feel lost when I feel divine guidance?
Perhaps because I want my clarity to come in visions
I want something concrete and leveled
I want to feel assurance within my knowing
It just needs to be powerful

I realize that most things are subtle
Just as the tears I shed daily
Frustration in my eyes as I continue in this passage
Looking to see, looking to find
This stranger within my mind

Carved into existence... an enigma
Images vague and obscure
The shadowing of its true aura
Who is this stranger in my mind?
I want to know, be of the know

I am only in transition because I don't wish to be
Annoying is this process of change
For I am impatient to wait for end results
Unsure inside my uncertainty
Where my doubts keep me in limbo

Shaded in the darkness lurking
Faceless, a vagabond whom longs permanency
A stabled land of existence
My inner soul searching...
I am the stranger within my mind

Time and Forgiveness

We sometimes doubt our abilities,
never truly knowing our own strength, until it shows up.

Death in our lives becomes a revealer...
showing us how vulnerable we really are.

Melting glacial coverings that seemed to mold our hearts,
reminding us of how much we actually can feel deep
within.

The memories reel in our heads like a slide show,
and the ones that departed us are featured with a smile.

How it seems their past offenses are of irrelevance...
and we would forgive them at the drop of a hat if only
they'd come back.

Making the minutest things...
seemingly even more obsolete,
and even truer... the statement, we can't pause time.

Time slips like fine sand through our fingertips
and there are no rewinds... no do-overs, it's from this point
on.

It begins to make you wonder...
do we remain mad at the world?
Or should we dig inside our better selves and make best of
today?

Becoming magnified, the little things of unimportance,
all the built-up anger without memory of where it derived.

Now wondering goes into a full circle of thoughts,
do we, could we, should we, why wouldn't we just move
forward?

How could we only pardon a loved one that is gone...
and why couldn't we grant the same forgiveness
to someone who's still here in the flesh?

Life becomes a bit easier, more bearable
when our hearts love again, open again...

We then can celebrate the here and now,
dissolving the past as we grant clemency to those in our
present.

Living in a day where most don't appreciate what they
have,
walking around scarred with other opened wounds.
It is not too late to begin anew... to change things in our
mirror,
nor too late, to adjust our prescribed seeing glasses.

Why would I begin to cast the first stone?
While here I am covered head to toe in rocks.

We all are worthy imperfections, original individuals...

so, let us not judge our fellow man, or harbor ill feelings

Let us not mourn our loss, with a what we should've
could've...
We can forgive today and wash their past away.

New starts and new beginnings, they happen every
millisecond
and now we can begin to be a part of that clock,
where time only ticks forward.

We don't want a life full of regrets...
it is up to us to utilize the time that we are here,
because it is so obvious...
that no one, not anybody,
can claim that they are promised tomorrow.

Let It Go

I grow silent
As I realize my voice is unheard
My latest actions
Speaks louder than explanations
Defending goes beyond reasoning
As exhaustion occurs

While the heart is seen
And intentions are at best
My actions are screaming
And all I can think is
Let it Go…

I become a priority,
Acknowledging that the normal exclusion of excuse
"To be human first"
That justification will not exempt
That we all must be held accountable
Blame will not falter and surely grow into unsound
character
So, to thyself be true
And hold on to truth
For the "Truth" shall set you free
Free!!!!
Free, to Let it Go…

I See You Brother!

I love the oomph in you,
That drive and determination...
That winning in your walk,
When you're filled with motivation

I like that confidence in your stride,
That self-assurance and poise...
Your truth voice that says listen
When you are surrounded in noise

I love the tall in your posture,
That long neck and head held high
And that you're polished in your dress,
These spells both Success & Fly

I love that you keep it positive
When the negativity begins to roll
And when other's ignorance goes viral
How you uphold your self-control

I love that your "gangsta'" means wisdom...
Not street cred by killing or selling drugs
And that you maintain respect,
By not looking or acting like a thug

I love the oomph in you,
That drive and determination...
That winning in your walk,
When you're filled with motivation

I love the go-getter mentality...
How "the man" doesn't keep you down
That your jar of excuses is empty...
And your good deeds are renowned

I can see you respect women,
Because your mother raised you well
Although she couldn't teach you how to become a man
Your father's absence, no one could tell

I love that you know your worth,
and it's not hidden on the bottom for you to see
And I love how you excelled
Although raised in poverty

I love your fortitude,
But that you are not afraid to cry...
And I love your empathy for others
A truly good guy, this implies

I see that you are a believer,
And that you pray each and every day
I love the GOD in you,
And how it's shown in every way

I see that you're not flashy,
Although you can easily afford
But that you rather give back,
Rebuilding your community is your reward

YES! I see you my strong distinguish brother,
Go ahead; I am so proud and of wonder
Despite all of your adversities
You wouldn't allow it... to... take you under!!!

In the Dark

Before I had not enough strength to fight
Or was it that I fought against the wrong cause
Because my insight wasn't that bright
Someone manage to switch out the light
And I was left in the dark
Alone to nurture this heart

Don't want to hurt others the way I hurt inside
Rather keep my pain isolated
Then to spread it out wide
This kind of misery truly does not love company
I left myself in the dark
Alone to cure this heart

Love's Absence

Love…
I try to reach you,
Stretching my heart beyond its limits
Knowing now, that it can never be
That all sense of reality has been captured
I don't want to hold you in this sacred safe place,
Because I rather be alone than to seek your face

Alone,
I try to stand,
Conquering this annoying thumping
In such an empty and hollow residence
This cold space on the other side of my bed
Lacking the silhouette of bod,
Where his chest, I was known to rest my head

Love…
Again, I ignore you,
Wish you were near, yet on the other hand
I curse your existence
Don't want to see the likes of you
Ask politely that you do not return
While I learn to accept the absence of you!

Alone,
Here I stand… Heart in hand
Burden by my past, the relationship that didn't last
I feel the healing begin
I realize that both the comfort and discomfort

Will soon dissolve;
Then where will I be?

Love…
I wish you were near
There I go with this confusion of placement
Beg you to leave, ask you than to stay
Just don't know how I feel today
I usually feed into the moment
But right now, I have no intent

Alone,
Tired of fighting/resisting you and this frustrating feeling
I've been there, done that, it's not quite appealing
Starve myself of love,
Just to feed its desires to you
So alone I stand
Repelling love's command

Love…
Please, stay away from me…
Do not expose me to your vulnerability
Once was blind, but now I see
That this heart can still function without you
Maybe (ALONE) is my destiny…
At least for now!

Alone,
Here I go again;

My own best and only friend
I fight you when times become longing
Right now, heart is cold, so I welcome you with opened
arms
But when the heat settles in,
I run to Love to breathe again!

Heartbeat

Listen to my heartbeat,
Can you translate the cryptogram?
That rapid thumping
As if it was to catch the last beat
Hurried… not haste…
The accumulating pace
The function
The treble
And the deep bass
The highs
The lows,
Of this junction
The erratic tones
The malfunction
Can you feel,
What I feel
For you
Do you
Understand
The code
Of my beating heart?

Ghetto Mentality Scheme

Once upon a time, it was proposed, projected and
schemed...
A plan to obliterate the black man's dreams

In all that is accessible within the land of the free
It was only but one that was prohibited, the forbidden tree

Made of strong trunk, deep rooted in knowledge
Branches that bear fruit from wisdom's college

Forewarned not to touch, eat or smell its harvest
Would be punished by genocide of those who are smartest

The brilliance of scholars would become distinct and no
more
By way of the ignorant beast that made wisdom their whore

That would rape her of her comprehension and cerebration
To stall a race with obliviousness and to end proliferation
of furthered education

It was forced and projected that this day no thoughts shall
they ever think
Not to ponder or reflect on their heritage... their greater
selves and legacies shall sink

No rapid eye movement and no futures for them to dream
This would become the land of the unconscious, which was
the plot and scheme

They would use "them" to hypnotize and mesmerize within
their musical decoding
Attached with it instructional videos of mastering the new
molding

Stripped of their birthright while housed in demographics
of poverty and segregation
Where the inner-city ghettos would be birthed and kept out
would be information

So, they plotted and executed their plan, first... within their
churches and temples
Replacing their Almighty with a monetary God, as if
praising materials and cars weren't that simple

This would impart resentment and jealousy for all that was
of luxury and of perceived riches
Then... renamed them degrading identities with mental and
physical carvings of "Niggas" and "Bitches"

And on their tubes... only Maury, Jerry Springer, and
reality TV shall be televised
So, they could be brainwashed of their worth because no
one was even wise to begin to realize

From crowns and royal robes, they degenerated to saggy
pants and the accentuation of flesh
No longer Congo drums stirring traditional rituals of
spiritual dance, it's now who can twerk the best...

They would share by way of the media and news, not of the
world, limited to only their neighborhoods
Spreading broadcast of negative imagery of only what was
familiarly seen, the part that was no good

And to add production, new development... how to keep
them in their place
Smuggling of drugs in their community to kill the morality
of the black man's race...

Set off by crime, prison cells, disease, social problems, lack
of resources and education
This project would be deemed the "ghetto mentality
scheme" to re-enslave the new generation

Tomorrow, Yesterday and Today

Tomorrow,
when the sun shines and rise,
leaving behind today and yesterday's sorrow
will it be so simple to forget the screams I hear in my
sleep?
will I only think them to be memories of a dream?

Yesterday,
it was the same ole thing,
lost within thoughts of the night before
or the night after, but never the night during
it is so easy to run away from today's reality!

Today,
I heard the echoes of the ambulance's sirens
bouncing off the walls in my bedroom,
must be the results of the screams I've ignored
the sun has barely kissed the morning sky and already
I want this day to end…

Destination Unknown

I pause…
I do not move forward, nor do I take steps backward
I take this moment to acknowledge my travels
Movement between pleasure and pain
I revisit the journey where travel was uncertain and a
destination,
damn... near... impossible!
I gave into the flow of things
feeling the wind beneath my feet
Pushing me closer to a breaking point
I gave and given all in which I held inside as sacred
I detoured to the ruins of our relationship,
closely capturing the past within view
How can one gain mileage to the future if they are
constantly looking back?
I took it as a voyage collecting clues to which way I would
transit next
It was a passage to growth
It was there,
That I found "truth", it was here, at this place…
Where I stopped and paused!

Look at Me, See Me!

Who I was, and who I am today, there are no regrets
Just nagging inclinations of what's to come

I am revealed in the nakedness of my soul,
I flaunt the nudity with a "look at me",
Look at me in all my bareness; can you see what I have
hidden?
Exposure carries no threat,
I can no longer hide behind the face that is masked...

My tear stained cheeks are now raw
Raw with my own guilt of encumbrance...
As my eyes were blackened by insomnia's burden,
Long nights of sleeplessness & streaming tears...

Such rarity when we bare ourselves
Going back to the basics of Adam and Eve
Before the evil serpent attacks
Before we realized our impurities
Even before our true forms became distinguished

My layers peeled back,
Opening self to be seen
Visuals of infected wounds
Gruesome toll to those who eye witnessed,
See me!
Beneath my skin structure,
The woman beneath the makeup...
Straight into my soul,

Beyond the windows
Where the shades are drawn

I challenge you... SEE ME!

Look at me,
Look at me and not straight through me,
See me,
See me as I show you
Revealing myself, my faults, my flaws and all...
In all my wrongness,
In the error of my ways,
I illustrate to you the good, the bad and the ugly
All due to my fallen and risen intentions...
In my flight and plummets,
I disclose to you,
Who I was, and who I am today
And all that there is left to say is...
Look at me... **see me!!!**

I Love My Ugly

Nowhere to run when in hiding from self
And while in darkness the torment of my own thoughts
They reel in the head as an autobiography of reminders…
This is who you are, and this is who you need to be

Inner conflict becomes a web of confusion
I've known this stagnant place well from memory
and yet, does pain rev up the nerves for change?
This is who I am, who do I need to become

We look for the drastic turning of events
Perhaps a reminder,
perhaps a truth serum of potent self-love
We search beyond the now as the distortion warps our
images…
But what if this is not a funhouse mirror,

What if… we see reflections of truth?

Try loving your ugly anyway!
Acceptance does not mean you like
We all sometimes feel that need, that desire to change
But let's face it; an upgraded model does not necessarily
equal improvement
So now, we are again in denial,
in hiding from this monstrosity
Can't stand the sight of our own reflection

Another reminder of the eyesore experiences
We have become what we've feared in the past
Turning ourselves into the truth of the lie
All in all is it more harmful what was said?
Or is it the self-perception of what was said?
In the end, we are our thoughts

Can we ever hide from them, our own?

Nowhere to run when in hiding from self
And while in darkness the torment of own thoughts
They reel in the head as an autobiography of reminders…
This is who you are, and this is who you need to be

I don't feel I look at change the same way
The word "change" has the appeal of wanting to be
something, someone else
I can only be me… I only desire improvement
No drastic metamorphosis, maybe peeling off layers

I don't want to cocoon myself until my core is damaged
Not only is there a newly realization of comfort in being
the way I am,
There attached is this contentment of I love my ugly
And there is always a way of improving

He Can Only Hold Her

Her fragile existence,
Demented mind,
Glacial cold-
Numbness self
SHATTERED!!!

Bearing the elements,
Blizzard-type
Freezing...
Unresponsive and
Detached!!!

Eyes that blankly
Stared at nothingness
Sought shadows,
Only recognizable
Images in her
State...

She dissipates
As she degenerates

Dissolving slowly
Sulking,
Slouching,
Hunched in pain
Named... "Insane"

Death reaping

On her breath
As she exhales
No more...
Inhales slightly,
Holding onto air...
BREATHE!!!
Damn it, breathe...

He holds her
Tightly,
For he can only
Hold her
So, he does...
Hold her
Embrace her
Squeezing her
She enfolds
She is holding on
She is feeling
And of feelings

She lives
In his arms
Collapsed and
Frail but...
She
Lives!

Chitter-Chatter

You don't even know it,
I suppose it doesn't even matter
All that chitter-chatter that
goes on in my mind.

My thoughts are consumed
of you. You take me under,
beneath the purifying waters
of your love. I'm drowning in
rivers of ecstasy and can't
catch my breath.

It's somewhere between an awe
and temptation, I can't say I'm in
this love, but each day I look for
you. Wishing that a touch
would kindle what my mind
won't hush about. No, this is
not infatuation, but it sure smells
of wilted roses.

It won't die inside, these thoughts
it lingers to blossom with the
reverse drought when you somehow
continue to refresh this thirst.

I close my eyes and I see you. I
don't want to sleep at night, in fright
that my dreams will lead beyond

fantasy and leave me yearning in
the morning.

We are so connected and yet you're
blinded and oh how I wish I was not
the only one with this vision. And then
there is the extinguisher to all this fire
burning inside. The fact that I am
already amid cinder passion.
How can two fires burn in one heart?

I can't explain to myself that I have
not created this; that I am not torn.
This heat is not a desire, I don't
long for you, or to be with you,
only to cradle you. How can
emotions wake me up at night,
leave me in fright and yet spark
a flame, that is always sweltering?

Can I ever say your name and not
feel tingles, not feel vibrations, not
feel you even in my fingertips?

I guess you don't even know it,
suppose it doesn't even matter
all that chitter-chatter that
goes on in my mind.

Love Poem to Jules #20

Somehow, I don't get it,
What draws me nearer to thee
What makes me desire you today,
More than I did yesterday?
How did we manage to stay so connected?
Then I realize as I am questioning myself
How much in love with you am I?
That I long to hear your voice… still
Still cuddling up inside your t-shirts entrenched with your sweat
And how it remains to drive me wild
Your scent…
Your touch…
Your love
It all keeps me coming closer
And I couldn't imagine my life without you
Or without your understanding
And patience
Your strong love and your drive
You are amazing…
And if I never get to tell you…
Read this poem!

Divinity's Pull

Softer thoughts greeted me this morn
My inner voice whispers reasoning
Says to me... give birth
Labor unto the world your gift
Share your shine

It's been time, time overdue
Time to no longer sleep on dreams
Where I once was fearful to acknowledge them
They grew faint within memory
Until I figured, I dreamed... not at all

It was sacred the way I raised out of bed
Focused attention to face a calling
Summoned by divinity's pull
I felt blessings had kissed my soul
As my spirit yearned no more

Peace became the sound of tapping on keys
Freedom was in each stroke
My mind mellowed itself of intent
As it became a slave to the screen
Every word stained a new beginning

Eyes wide opened to see this world differently
A greater vision beyond boxed contemplations
It was no longer about the selfishness
Not about cheapened self-pleasuring with mental
stimulation

It correctly developed into motivated elevation of the art

Softer thoughts greeted me this morning
An internal peace that spoke truth
That opened my eyes a little wider
The elimination of the mask, a truth caller
Today I saw myself for the first time as a writer

Trance

Your eyes penetrate my soul
Speaking freely to my heart
While making love to my memory

I am caught in your trance
Gasping for air
For my breath, you stole
With your kiss

Your smile indulges me
It ignites inner warmth
Makes my knees weak

I am caught in your trance
Your spirit moves me
Pulls and leads me
In love's direction
It speaks to my heart

Fading

Have I ever told you?
That you remind me of the flowers
The ones I saw on the way
Along the roadside
They were delicate
Beautiful, sweet scented
And yet, slumped over

You used to remind me
Of the wheat
We used to pass
Standing tall and strong
You were nourishing
Pretty to the eyes
Refreshing

What has happened to you?
You are slowly withering away
You're so cold
And malevolent
Even still, I see courage
I see it in your eyes
I know that one day,
Soon, you will stand tall again

Have You Ever?

Ever get lost...
inside your mind, as you search
to find your way out of it
of the confusion,
of the self-deception
out of the embedded suffering...
ever get lost?

Ever had inner tricks played...
where you're stern, yet unsure
confident, but insecure
happy, and yet sadness flows
stable as you lose control

Ever imagined peace...
in your disordered being
blinded by the light
yet forever seeing
your inner message... still deceiving
but in fact, the truth,
you are incessantly receiving

Ever want to know
while still living in doubt
locked in your confinement
peeking out the window
stepping one foot out the door
one step closer to freedom
but fears contagiously spread

so, you stay inside instead

Ever just release
to find yourself in inner-peace
Ever just hope
as you trust yourself enough to cope
Ever just live
stop taking and just give
Ever believed,
the whispering thoughts that you received
Ever, have you ever just prayed?
and left it there...

Have you ever just come to be?
Despite others perception of your identity
Have you dared to see your true reflection?
while listening to your inner echo
listening to your heart's rhythm
listening to your thoughts churn
and inside you burn to learn...
why so absent
why so much misunderstanding
why so much of why being asked?

Ever just set yourself free
tuning inside your harmony
listening to the melody
creating the song of your life
lyrical blessings of love

Ascending above... taking flight
heading towards the light
where true independence resides
outside of the circular thought
ever just find yourself there caught
caught in the moment
caught in this instance of now
knowing all there is to know of self

Ever just unpacked
letting go of layers of burdens
letting go
letting go
just letting go
as learning to appreciate the way life flows
just wanted to know...
Have you ever?

A Dirt Path

I have bricked many unpaved roads
The first to travel the lined cement

Many sectors detoured
Outcomes unplanned
Fate has many options
Yet the shining golden stone road does not appeal

I love to gallop over the pot holes
Ditch and dodge the cracks
Seems the harder the journey, the greater the reward

I rather earn from sweat and tears
Then it be simple
Leaving me left unfulfilled
Or feelings of unworked

If it's too easy, believe me
I don't want that way
Give me a dirt path
And see what I have
By the end of the day

She's Strong!

I admire her strength
How she keeps on keeping on
Damn, she's strong
but for how long?

'Cause we all need our rest
Rest sista rest, I suggest
you need time to digest
the world is not feeding you their very best
so rest, sista rest!

I'm so impressed
How she maintains
Her pain, she contains
and then let it flow in her nightly tears
Headstrong, and relaxed of fears
my dear sista,
I admire her so

There is fire in her eyes
amazing determination,
And a luster for life
there is no hesitation
with her flirtation
as she is intimate with living

Heart so pure and giving

Damn she's driven

look at her conquering her goals
one by one she tackles obstacles
There must be super in her flyness
Greatness in her divineness
A pure role model of one that is truly blessed

but I still say...
rest my sista rest

She's full-blooded regal
Royalty In veins, she is Queen
beautiful skin of vanilla bean
she's damn right gorgeous
especially when her alluring spirit is seen
She's sight of a dream
But the force that is with her
She's that well-oiled machine

I admire her strength
How she keeps on keeping on
Damn, she's so strong
Solid and resilient
Beautiful mind, attractive spirit...
My lovely sista,
and I appreciate her so!

Your Lies

Your Lies began my confusion
And I am at war…
Mesmerized by the ties
That continuously bond, you and I

In my sleep, I claim defeat
Hypnotic by your view
Intellectual symptoms stimulate
What few could appreciate

I caught your sarcasm virus,
Only a handful escaped
But I stayed caught up in your mind game

A fist full of illusions,
From your twisted and contorted conclusions…
This is how your Lies began
…my confusion

Reach Me

Say to me the words longing outside range of my
vocabulary
And understanding
Reach my heart beyond the pearls of my existing loins
I am not the soulful mixture of tampered regales
I am not the vixen in the videos

I am not the one that desires the affection of your lust
Speak to me

Say things that are unheard from these ears
Un-virgin my mind… be my first
Pronounce with the utter of your voice the way I should
feel
Thus, feel with me

Reach me… teach me how to interpret your love language
Lure me with a dialect so sweet
Tender me, tender me… tender me!

Roots

Our mothers are sisters,
Bonded in love by the womb they shared
Connecting and fused by one upbringing
We are the product of our mothers
As they are of their mother

We are cousins,
Yet raised as sisters
My love outreaches the stretches of the earth,
The one that I have for you

You and I learned a secret lingo,
In which we used to conduct cherished conversations
We share a past, and yet, our futures spread like branches
As adults now, we bear fruit

The same structural foundation that we were raised from,
Our grandmother's trunk,
The core of this family,
Her wisdom spreads to us within her twigs

As we sprout our own branches…
We grow as our children grow
Bigger and stronger… and more firm
And what our mothers have taught
They too shall learn

The Desert is Calling

Without a trace of moisture,
The dry crystals of rocks and minerals absorbs the heat
Crying out for one drop to ease the burning
Parched are its dusty crusted layers
I hear the desert land calling for my tears

My skin glistening from sun kisses
My head is in a spin of distraught
The earth is listening...
Anticipating my emotional outpour

The air is thick,
Firm without humidity

Again... the dessert is calling
Calling for my tears
Desperately pleads for my soul to moan its release
"You know you want to weep my child," it says
"Help me, by helping you"

"Sprinkle me with your pain" it solicits

My brow shows traces of concern
Discomfort for the gravel as well as my own wellbeing
My mother earth has nurtured me long with her beauty
Her nourishments have kept me
Preserved me in physical health
As she pleads, I identify

My emotions are stirring...
A sensation transfer and embodies itself
I feel droplets of pain aching for release

I will provide as she has provided for me

One lonely tear isolated
And many more to follow as if it was rehearsed
I hear the desert calling for more
I hear her sigh in relief
I hear her calling...
The desert is calling

A Glimpse of Hope

Sometimes inspiration is needed
Just a glimpse of hope
A light
An inner glow acknowledged
It all does something to the spirit

Cherished are my thoughts
The positive that keeps me moving

Always in search for peace
And when I find her... she breathes through me
Inhaling, exhaling her essence
She takes hold of me
Takes control of my worries
And eases this troubled mind

Hope is something I blanket myself inside
I love her warmth, her comfort
The way she speaks to me
And the conveying of her tranquility

My most thought provoking moments
Are when I dare to challenge my depression
The sternness of my determination to rid myself of it
Declaring a war on my inner darkness

Courage is always required
My fears will never debilitate my ambition of me keep on
keeping on

For we all must stay strong

Courageous is the one who refuses
Refusal of lying down helplessly
Hell, no, I won't go to the other side willfully
I will not surrender myself to the hold of deceit

When in darkness... always face the light
Because sometimes inspiration is needed
Just a glimpse of hope

Impact

Her screams...
Her screams echoed off walls
Ricocheted across rooms
The piercing sound… made the dead rise
The sleep… conscious
And the annoyed, justified!

Her state of mind was of destruction
She fell into a hurt that graved
Torn…
Between her heart and mind
Was paranoia a fable of reminders?
Was his truth a suicidal bomb?
How could little words
Make such an explosive impact

Eyes red and barely opened
Her tears were a stream
Creating ripples of emotions
Life changed in an instant
Her happy life was now in the past
Her world stopped turning
She rocked in a dire motion
Noted in mind…
"Pain cannot be this painful"

Dreading her next thought
She shuts down completely
Her head hangs lifeless upon her knees

As she continues to rock
Her motion more violent
Staring into dead air
Feeling lifeless emotions
She rocks…
She rocks,
She rocks…

How could life do this to her… again
Another stressful traumatic occurrence
How could God do this to her again
Another test in life
That she could have not possibly studied for
Another trial
Where she felt, she was convicted
Another unfair sentenced
It was life's karma boomeranging…

She was burning within the ember flames of her mind
Felt like hell on earth
Veins in her arms and head resembled a map
Protruding and throbbing….
Suffering would not be an option…. But mandatory
As her soul quakes
And body shakes
She trembles within own self
Her silence would be no more…
She rocks…
She rocks,

She rocks…

Her long line of sexual abuse
Her long line of misuse
She refused to let it change her
So badly she wanted to switch gears
But her heart held its hold
Strongly willed to not touch her madness
Insanity would befall, and come in trances
Violence could be stemming
Her rude awakening came with his apology
Her motions slowed… then ceased
Her woe is me turned into disgust

Rage was an inferno burning inside
Rapidly the fire grew
She had little restraint to her momentary insanity
Fast paced, she jumps up and slaps his face repeatedly
He stood there and took each smack
One after another
The one blow she placed all strength in,
He caught her hand, and held it stiff

No more words would be exchanged…
Only a soft peck from him, to her brow
And then he left

Read My Mind Part III

He buried himself into the comprehension of my soulful
meaning
Deciphering the sight, sound, and touch with care and
attention
He was extremely mindful when it came to my desires
Reading my mind precisely…

His interpretations of my emotions were with an impressive
glowing touch
Together we shared a confidential and detailed moment

He gratified me with the indulgence of sweet conversation
We shared intimacy through words
He moved me… slowly… with intensity… and bathed me
within metaphors
Sentiments of devotion, enhanced with real emotion,
He had me singing inside my head, songs of admiration

Brotha had the aura of temptation
Stimulants of his understanding gave both fever and chills
Wow! I sent out a request, and he obliged.
Every aspect and expectation reached,
He had me lost within his speech… he was ready to teach,
And I, I was so ready to learn, eager to become an
apprentice

Flowing from his lips was this cognitive awakening
He had planted this mental seed
I had to massage my own temples,

For the formation of mental objects, we erected,
And I felt at home, even as thoughts roamed

So, trivial, yet profound, this confusion within my search,
Just for someone to Read My Mind!

How Do I Begin?

How can I begin, to be honest with myself?
When ambiguity is the reject effect of truth
My mind tries earnestly defeating unsound reasoning
With introduction to Whom, What, When, Where and
Why…
Who is it that I am?
What is it that I want?
When will this come to fruition?
Where do I begin?
And why haven't I already begun asking these questions?

To search;
Not just seeking with mind,
But to quest deeper into soul,
Listening closely to the spirit answers
Meditating with an unabridged heart
Lurking within the crevices of doubt, to destroy hesitation's
existence
Liveliness of action… soul's reaction… mind's satisfaction
No more stumbling at life's door… knocking
Every entrance has opened with possibilities

Never limiting my blessings by counting, them
Acknowledging the sacred signs and good deeds as God's
gifts
This has become life altering
For I have laid my burdens down
Discharging the confusion of unmentionable strife
Conflictions of the mind tortures souls

I had to let go, I had to release… I had to ascend above
So, that I may begin, to be honest with myself

I feel that we are our own gardeners
The WORD is a knowledgeable book of guidance
The How-To(s) and Instructions to nurture your life-force
The assistance to attain results of spiritual growth
Brooding hate will only eliminate and destroy
Its intentions are toxic to the progression you wish to see
Your transformation will not manifest into merits
Perhaps turn into the likeness of torture on Earth
Our souls cry for its rebirth…
For it wants to be renewed!

So how can I begin, to be honest with myself?
If I do not channel inside
Become intimate with my secret longings
And the initiator of the termination of my own suffering
Purge myself with confessions and of digressions to rectify
How can I begin, to be honest with myself?
If I continuously do not search inward, and outwardly live a
lie
Now studying at the institution of Whom, What, When,
Where and Why…
As I discover the truth about life!
My life… without limitations of just trying to reach the
sky!

Love's Light

Let love be the light
That guides us,
Let its warmth
Melt our hearts
And take away
The coldness of pain
Let us love again
Let us love again
Let us…
Know again…
The light of love!!!

Memories

Her forgetfulness imposes worries
Time locked away in a vault
Inaccessible to her
The most valuable of memories
Remote and replaced with vagueness

How could all the bad remembrance stay?
The mind will not grant access to happier moments
It's like fine sand slipping through fingers
The tighter she grasps
It escapes her completely

She studies the scrapbooks
She remembers the photos,
Although not the memories attached
Someday it shall all come back to her
She hopes as she studies harder

Told by loved ones that she has them
To live in the moment of now...
Brows raised and nosed turned up
She queried...
"And what about the ones that are gone?"

That would always have silenced them
They knew not how to answer such question
For they've been told of condolence
"You always have your memories"
For the one without, what would they say?

My Kind of Misery Don't Like Company

Sometimes I feel the heat against my neck
And fatigue all over my body,
My soul just aching for some peace
Here I am smothering myself within a blanket of blues
Cozy all up in this foolishness

Dealing with the disturbances inside my mind
All this commotion of ups and downs
Life's sudden surprises and not so quaint experiences
Don't need one feeling sorry for me
Heck, not even an ounce of shame
Trust me; I don't enjoy being where I am
Alone, and somewhat grumpy
But don't you bother knocking at my door
My kind of misery don't like company

See, I've been in this dark place
Closed shades and closing of the mind
Been bathing in my heartache
Or pouring out my pain
But let me tell you something...

I do not wish to transfer this negativity
I don't wish my pain to rub off on you
And while you are smiling and living your life
I'm not about hoping to see you fail
I pray that you prosper in all that you do

Cause, I'm the kind to wish you well

I love to see other's blessings come through
I attempt to motivate and to inspire
And even when I am down like this
I want to see you go higher

My heart is designed to feel another's pain
Imagine the intensity felt of my own
Sometimes I'm just in the land of the lost
And need to shut off the ringer to my phone
I'm comforted within my own cozy bed
This big down pillow while trying to receive my rest
But I am not about to call you up
To have you witness me at my lowest

I'll do my best to mask with a smile
Suffering in silence, I can't help myself
But if you ask, sometimes I do need to vent
Most times I won't… and if I do it is reluctantly
You see my kind of misery don't like company

I don't want you to take one step in my shoes
Don't want you to feel the funk in my blues
And if I'm broken and torn apart
You best believe it makes good art
Because my pain I bleed as I ink my heart
Believe me, I am okay

And if by chance you do not hear from me suddenly
A long drought between conversations
Perhaps I've been a bit sadden
And busy with prayer and meditation
Don't you go worrying for me!
You see,
My kind of misery just don't like company

Laid Back Brotha

I like a laid back brotha
With leaned back posture like no otha
The kind that will small talk you straight into big ideas
The ones he gives for free yet you are tempted to steal
You know the brotha with his pockets low
But hold high expectations
Never flaunt what he knows
Yet it's something he gently expose

I like his unkempt beard and faded sneakers
His tattered threads but he's a keeper
Because he's a believer
Of all things being possible, even when it's impossible
When I'm with him I feel so unstoppable
He keeps me dreaming when I am afraid to sleep
And he sows in life, ten times that he reaps

I like a motivated brotha
With mystique to uncover
His charisma and aura is like no otha
Brilliant and gifted,
Strong and uplifted,
Wise beyond his years and appearance
Built with both purpose and perseverance
I love how he conquers and then defeats
And how he learns from his errors without repeats

Oh, I like that focused with drive type brotha
The kind that earns respect from mothers
Because he's a gentleman and God-fearing
Most respectable from his rearing

Cool, calm and collective but rough around the edges
Remains the same of whatever he alleges
That laid-back posture without a worry
A man with a past, but glory in his story!
A rebel against society's expectations, and yet he is
A successful man, because the way he lives

Judgmental Eyes

I find it hard to look at others with judgmental eyes,
Too much self-judgment upon myself
Yet I learn to place those discernments upon a shelf
And storage the love inside myself

Oh this woman's worth far more than riches
No negativity attached, no dreams or wishes
I live the life I want, at this moment in time... right now
I didn't believe I could, but I showed me how

Love for self can make one disregard the darkness
Cherish the happiness and live a life of bliss
When I walk no longer a slump; but a raised head
In those dark and back allies, I no longer tread

Armored with a spirited self-esteem and even stronger faith
In my looking glass, I no longer dissipate
I am looking at her, at me... at us... at we
The gentle and warmth that set us free

Yes, my lovely self, her and I... she and me
We marched a purposeful trail to our destiny
I find it hard to look at others with judgment at all
I don't look down on others; I'm just not that tall

Pretty Girl with Issues

For so long I have been the pretty girl with issues
But before you reach for your tissues, do not pity me
I am the epitome,
Of survival
I overcome and thrash demons…
As they try to rape me and inject their semen,
Inside these walls of my peace

And believe it or not
It's perseverance within their mind corruption
That tries to claim destruction within me
But cannot have me, they will not
Win over me

I've protected myself from day one
Armored with prayer and managing... with my passion
It gives me more than satisfaction
All because...
Freedom rings in pen's pressing sound made on paper

It was through POETRY that I learned how to save "her"

Writing became just as vital as the daily nutrition my body
needs
It became the abortion of the demons' implanted seeds
A way to rid myself of the insanity
Staying true to my humanity and gaining new self-worth
It was death to the issues and to Elle... a rebirth

My art was a self-portrait
I used my words to paint only what was seen to self
Deterioration of the mind struggles with my health
And yet...
The words were relevant within the moment
The way it captured my past... then release
Detection of the pain, then relief
It was my heart wide open and worn on my sleeve
And fed me moments that I could believe...

Yes, I am a Survivor

For so long I have been the pretty girl with issues
But before you reach for your tissues, do not pity me
I am the epitome,
Of survival
I overcome and thrash demons…
As they try to rape me and inject their semen,
Inside these walls of my peace

With pen in my hand,
My nights are long…
Sometimes impossible to not consent
I am here in the present
But absent

There is a blockage and a blankness
A tightly held pen, I caress
And then I write…

Some recommend me to reach deeper
Deep into that dungeon-ness place
They say...
Seek your true face,
In truth, you will be that grand reaper
Killing the torture that is embedded
And no doubt I will invoke up more pain
They say...
Feel it, and don't regret it

And once you hit a nerve,
Keep going, they say
You're headed…
In the right direction
When thoughts reach
An excited erection
You've found your perfection
And ink
Ink before you think

Let it burn the pages

For so long I have been the pretty girl with issues
But before you reach for your tissues, do not pity me
I am the epitome,
Of survival
I overcome and thrash demons…
As they try to rape me and inject their semen,
Inside these walls of my peace

Sometimes I pray...
I truly do every day... but sometimes I PRAY!
And let the spirit take over
There are moments when I just let my inner-self speak to
the rest of me
The struggle with immoral and the best of me
Other moments I am hanging on by a thread
So, I hang on to what's left of me
Begging GOD to show me my destiny
AND then I praise! In so many ways
Releasing the tears, I held in so many days

I was once enslaved
My emotions concaved
Directed inward, the negativity
Lowered self-esteem and hypersensitivity
My response to life was undesirable
Embedded blame within my heart
And refusal of forgiveness

Always taking it out on paper
Armored with pen in hand
And unfinished memoirs with a long line
Of to be continues….
More than a life full of experience in such a short time
Pen reloaded in ink,
Pressed against paper even harder this time

For so long I have been the pretty girl with issues

But look at me…
I survived!!!
I am alive, and I am living…
Beyond just prevailing
And though there are still visual scars,
I AM HEALED!!!
There is an appeal to being angry still,
But to reveal the past was to release the past

Forgiveness was my healing agent
The past buried beneath the pavement
The same path I trudge on was...
Rerouted and redirected in a new direction
Where imperfection has become my perfection
As my pen shout,
And it releases it all out…
I can truly say,
In this day,
I am no longer a pretty girl
But a beautiful woman

No longer slumped when I stand
Still armored with pen in hand
But when I write…
It's about the flight,
Elle's escaped plight

My testimony…
Is in my ink

It's in my bleed
It's in the toner
It's stained on paper

And

I no longer want to erase her…
The pretty girl with issues…
But release her abuse
Release her misuse
Release her…
For she was my muse,
The pretty girl with issues!

Epilogue

Shantelle 'Elle' McLin

About the Author

Raised in one of the most influential cities in the United States history, Shantelle 'Elle' McLin was born on Thanksgiving Day in 1975. In a thriving city, home of the first automobile and the musical movement of the new genre sound of Motown, Elle was the second conceived of three in a family of all daughters. Managing to stay an honor student during difficult setbacks, after a short break, she would become a graduate of "The Breakfast Club" program in MI. Shantelle soon after would attend Oakland Community College studying Liberal Arts.

Recreational writing began for this author at the age of 9 in journal formatting. Her creativeness was sparked in Middle school during a notable visit to the library with her best friend. With an outdated range of selections, she instantly identified with the poets' generations before her; she had found her outlet. While facing great personal difficulties, Elle treated poetry as a feel-good remedy to her melancholic episodes. This would become freeing to a young and timid adolescent, as she discovered her voice. Writing would become a soother and her pen, a microphone to express her challenges.

In 2009, several decades and many poems later, Shantelle would be given an opportunity to showcase her literary expressions and love for the written arts. As a gift from a first cousin her website **www.ellemclin.com**, (A Shared

Format 4 Poets) would be initiated. One year later her first publishing opportunity would present itself in an anthology "Eros 369", several of her works were featured there. In 2013, this poetess would be introduced to a publisher with Inner Child Press. Elle's first book of published poems was created. "My First Poetry Book", a chapbook. Featured in many online Poetry magazines as well as webcast radio shows where she would recite and share her work.

Besides poetry, Author McLin's second passion is photography, where she loves to spotlight the innocence of children in her work.

Elle resides in her hometown of Detroit, MI. with her husband, daughter, and mother.

Book Description

Between the covers of this book you will find a pilgrimage.

For author, 'Elle' McLin, in describing her past as a painful one, would be trite and dismissive. It is through enormous turmoil that she found herself; slowly healing, then breaking free of victimhood. She later awakens to new found hope.

A victim of sexual abuse; the reality of her writing conveys to the reader, that the true assault was the violation of her soul. The aftermath was a skewed self-perception, which created a pattern of self-deprecation and bitter angst. This is a glimpse into the heart of a woman who became terrified of love, yet desired to be loved; a dichotomy.

So skillfully written, Elle has masterfully conveyed her deepest, blood-raw emotions in this exquisite collection of prose. It will be an emotional journey you take with her, feeling each inference, innuendo and breath. It is a tale of inner strength, fortification and a woman reinvented. The author has discovered self-love; the key was never outside of herself. A victory for this very brave, strong woman.

Walk this pilgrimage with 'Elle." You will find seeds enough to plant within yourself! Powerful and evocative - not to be missed.

Brenda-Lee Ranta – Author of *Myriad of Perceptions & Allegories*